The Growth Imperative

Reimagining the future of work

Jack Ricchiuto

~ DesigningLife Books ~

Books by Jack Ricchiuto

Collaborative Creativity / 1996

Accidental Conversations / 2002

Project Zen / 2003

Appreciative Leadership / 2005

Mountain Paths / 2007

Conscious Becoming / 2008

Instructions From The Cook / 2009

The Stories That Connect Us / 2010

The Enchantment Of Casual Origins / 2011

The Joy Of Thriving / 2012

Ordinary Eyes / 2012

The Agile Canvas Field Guide / 2012

Abundant Possibilities / 2013

The Power Of Circles / 2013

Making Sense Of Time / 2014

Beyond Recipes / 2014

Focus / 2015

Smarter Together / 2015

Ideas / 2015

The Art Of Conversations / 2016

The Way Of Questions / 2017

The Growth Imperative / 2018

3 | The Growth Imperative

The Growth Imperative

Reimagining the future of work

Jack Ricchiuto
DesigningLife Books
1020 Kenilworth Avenue
Cleveland OH 44113 USA

ISBN 978-1983426117
Paperback

I.   Title
1. Human potentials. Organization development.
Workplace change. Teambuilding. Leadership.

First edition, January 15, 2018
Printed in the USA

Production: CreateSpace
Cover: Tia Andrako

Content

Business as unusual

Growing together

Realizing our potential

Engagement

The future of growth

Invitation

What's becoming more clear to those of us working with organizations across industries and continents is the profound distinction between nimble and slow teams. It's in their relationship to uncertainty.

While slow teams resist uncertainty as a threat to comfort zones, nimble teams practice the natural and ancient wisdom of oysters. When an oyster encounters some form of uncertainty, it transforms it into a magnificent and priceless pearl.

Nimble teams flourish because they know how to transform uncertainty into the gem of growth.

This is a series of meditations on changing the conversation about the future of work. It is an invitation to explore together the possibility and power of doing work where the point and path is growing together. My intention is to spark new conversations.

Jack Ricchiuto
January 2018

Business as unusual

The future of work

Imagine a world where work is a place of meaning, community and joy.

It's already happening. In margins of improbability, people around the world are reimagining workplaces where they feel valued, connected and free to grow.

It's happening where the most worthy and rewarding purpose of work is growing together. When we grow together, we flourish together on all levels of narratives and numbers. We become richer human beings.

We are the humble yet relentless disrupters of business as usual that continues to keep the vast majority of people, over 80% globally, working with low levels of engagement and passion.

We are the imagineers working at right angles to what our industrial predecessors did back in the day. With no stone unturned, we experiment with anything we can. No conventional practice is off the table of reimagining the potential of work.

We want to get work right. We don't believe work needs to be the last place people want to be. We believe the future of work holds more promise than its past holds destiny.

We believe work can be an inspiring place where we can discover, engage and celebrate our good and goodness. We believe workplaces can be rich networks of purpose, practice and perspective. We believe work can be a vibrant context for the kind of efficacy that enriches every other dimension of our personal paths.

We are the nimble who know that in new conversations about the future of work, the declared impossible, once again, becomes possible.

'Tis a gift to be nimble

Whether we're talking about work in global corporations, small businesses or public sectors, organizations are dynamic networks of teams. Each team performs along a continuum between nimble and slow.

On nimble teams we are aspired, responsive and connected. We are aspired by our desire to realize the good we want to see. We are responsive to each new opportunity to make good possible. We are connected in clarity of the good we seek and the goodness we are. These make us nimble. We grow together.

Slow teams are awkward, risk-averse and cautious. They are awkwardly unsure if what they're doing is approved or valued. They are risk-averse in resisting growth because of the intrinsic uncertainties in growth curves. They are cautious when things happen unplanned.

The difference in teams is culture. In nimble cultures, our priority is on growing together. Growing is opening up to new kinds of clarity in the possibilities of our work, our lives and our world. Every new kind of significance, contribution and connections in our work comes about because we have opened to new kinds of clarity. Each shift turns uncertainty into an asset.

In slow cultures, the priority is on working by permission. Over 90% of leaders still operate from the practices from command and control. People do what they have approval to do. Closed to anything else, they don't grow.

Nimble teams outperform slow because we make growing together the point and path of our work. It takes us an hour to do what it takes slow teams 6-8 hours to do. This is the power of shared clarity.

The vast majority of organizations worldwide are more on the slow end of the tempo continuum. They struggle to make their numbers because without a culture of growth, they cannot move beyond the invisible fence of their status quo.

No team becomes greater by permission. Each becomes greater through shared dedication to the constancy of growing together.

The growth imperative

In nimble teams our growth is inspired by the good we seek together.

What's good is the beauty we want to contribute to our world. It's the best possible future we want to create for the wellbeing of all. It's our deepest wishes for our planet. It's the progress we can make toward the realization of these.

Our sense of good has power precisely because we define it together.

Our sense of good is always aspirational, aligned and agile along the way. Always evolving, the good we seek two quarters from now will be different from how we think of it today. It's what we move toward rather than against. It's what we want more rather than less.

In traditional language, good can be expressed in vocabularies of mission, vision, values, strategy, goal, objective, metric and standard. In more poetic, nimble culture terms, we talk about good in the language of dream, passion and beauty. Each is simply some form of what we consider good.

On nimble teams, every conversation we have is shaped by what we consider good. The simplicity of "What would be good here?" frames our clarity.

We create good by engaging our goodness. We feel valued, connected and free to grow.

Goodness is the chemistry of abilities and qualities that makes good possible. These include our personal, social, psychological, practical, technical, creative and spiritual abilities and qualities like curiosity, persistence, focus, presence, adaptability and compassion. We grow by engaging our goodness.

We open to new kinds of clarity about the good we seek through the synergies of our abilities and qualities. Symbiotically, growing our abilities and qualities makes new kinds of clarity more possible.

Growing has no formal curriculum or calendar. It's woven throughout the fabric of work. We don't sign up for it. We aren't mandated to it. It happens in every conversation, project and shift. Our unequivocal commitment to growing personally and together becomes more a matter of identity than assignment.

There is a social benefit side to the equation. Growing in our work makes growth more possible in our lives. When we grow through our work, we become better partners and parents, friends and families, community members and citizens. When we grow, everything grows.

It's time to start talking about how to reimagine work for the possibility of a growth imperative.

Through a dark lens, slowly

In contrast to the brilliant perspective of nimble teams on good and goodness, slow teams maintain a darker lens on what's wrong and what they lack. Their habits of awkwardness, risk-aversion and caution have a reciprocal relationship to a negative focus.

They sincerely believe a dark lens is key to a brighter future. Their confusion about flourishing keeps them slow.

Instead of putting their attention on the good they seek and the goodness they have, they dwell on conflicts, tensions, gaps, deficiencies, failures, disappointments, dramas, grievances, criticisms, complaints, dislikes, hates, worries, threats, risks and fears.

This confusion is exactly what keeps them working at low levels of engagement and passion.

When they stop this insanity, they move easily and quickly toward more moments of nimble. We have so many stories of the worst performing teams in organizations becoming the best simply by shifting their focus. All the research points to this.

If anyone on a slow team went to their manager one morning and said, "Look, I've seen all the data, and I just want you to know I will no longer entertain conversations here about our deficiencies and what's wrong," by early afternoon they would find themselves busy on a LinkedIn search.

There's nothing wrong with naming things problems and weaknesses. A nimble focus isn't a denial of what's wrong and what we lack. We are acutely and realistically aware of both. We just know there is no evidence that we grow from negativity.

Focus on bad is based on the confusion that good is the elimination of bad. So much good in our world happens because people focus on the good they want and the goodness they have rather than on what they think is wrong and weakness.

The first cell phone innovators who globally transformed communication, learning and commerce dedicated zero time to first trying to get rid of all the landline phones, libraries, file cabinets, faxes, mailboxes or brick and mortar stores.

Creating good is a completely different strategy than waging war on bad. From a design perspective, everything performs the way it's designed to perform. Inspired by good, we design our way into the world we want to see.

The beauty of good

Since the beginning of time, language defines the way we live and work. As we grow, our language shifts, our sense of clarity shifts.

Nimble people describe good in the poignant language of love, dreams and beauty. We talk about what we would love to see possible. We dream far out into the future beyond the constraints of self-interest and risk-aversion. We frame beauty as the ultimate lens of good.

Our tempo is energized by the quality of our questions. We are most inspired by the more beautiful questions. What's the beauty we want to see and create? What would be beautiful success and progress? What would be a most beautiful atmosphere to work in and from? How could what we're working on be more beautiful?

Every kind of work becomes awe-inspiring craft when it's about creating beauty in what we do and how we do it. Beauty is not the exclusive domain of aesthetics. We can talk equally about the beauty of things that work well.

When beauty is our focus in work, we work with care, kindness and love. What we do matters. What we create has significance. We get more energy from work than we give to it. Beauty is the ultimate antidote to burnout.

The simple and powerful attention to beauty as a prime consideration of the good we seek expands our capacity for imagination and courage. Beauty is a compelling lens for seeing good with the newness of fresh eyes. It uniquely brings about a new clarity about good. It evokes our goodness.

Work as craft

When we are clear that good is beauty our work becomes a craft. We infuse our work with new kinds of clarity. We grow together.

Four things make work a craft.

- It is a craft when we think we can get better at it.
- It is a craft when the details of process and product matter.
- It is a craft when the standards we have for ourselves are higher than those others have for us.
- It is a craft when we use mindfulness to make it happen.

When work is a craft, we give attention to how things work and feel. We include in our definition of any good how simple and satisfying things are. It doesn't matter what we produce and deliver in our work, anything can be simple and satisfying. We have a natural human trust of things we find beautiful.

When we work from a craft mindset, work is always interesting. We're always trying new things. Our pride in what we do is priceless.

It's all about the numbers, except when it isn't

The conversation about beauty is profoundly distinct from the conversation about numbers.

Nimble teams know their numbers. We just don't obsess over them the way slow teams do. We know numbers are the lag symptoms of the lead, causal factor of culture. Culture is what makes strategy and structure work.

Numbers come from culture. When we get culture right, we get the numbers right. We get culture right when working is about growing together. Realizing good is more about sociology than numerology.

Before we get this, we put pressure on people for their numbers. We superstitiously believe that pressure applied well in the past was responsible for people making their numbers. When we don't get culture, we have no idea where the numbers actually come from and what pressure actually does.

The latest research about the relationship between pressure and performance indicates that when we feel pressure for performance, the creativity and collaboration networks in our brains shut down.

The more we stress from pressure, the more we work with a fixed mindset, making us reluctant to grow much less grow together.

Pressure makes us risk averse and more prone to the safe, approval based, slow cultures. All of this adds up to a glass ceiling on performance that not even expensive threats and bribes can overcome. Every slow culture has some nimble people. In slow cultures, the nimble few work overtime.

Team detox

In living systems, toxicity threatens and inhibits growth.

In human systems, toxic energy is denying the goodness in others and ourselves. We deny goodness by obsessing on weakness.

Most people on slow teams would find it incredible that people on nimble teams don't spend time talking about each other's weaknesses. People on nimble teams find it incredible that growing together could ever happen in a toxic culture of denying each other's goodness.

Toxic energy manifests in different grades. High grade toxicity is active or passive forms of hostility, bullying, disregard and rude. Middle grade is trust-depleting gossip, complaining, criticism and dismissing. Low grade is mindlessly going through the motions, box checking and trying to get out of anything new. Each is a different level of confusion.

Anything a teams does to illuminate anyone's goodness detoxifies the culture, making everyone more ready and able to grow.

Because of our neuroplastic brains, everyone can cultivate the ability to see goodness in themselves and others.

Nimble teams neutralize toxicity by boosting their cultural immune system. We do this by dominating conversations with talk of the good we are creating and the goodness engaged in the process.

Bringing out each other's goodness

One of the more natural, sustainable and connecting ways of opening to new clarity about each other's goodness is through storytelling.

Nimble teams regularly create time in conversations for sharing current and past stories of successes achieved, obstacles overcome, problems solved, lessons gleaned from experiments and experiences. Each reveals new insights into the goodness at the table. We especially do this when new people join the team and when we're working with other teams for the first time.

We stay largely unconscious of each other's goodness if we assume the only goodness that exists is the goodness we have already seen.

Whatever their generation and gender, everyone comes to the table with all manner of unseen goodness.

Each of us has our own constellations of qualities and abilities, no two of us exactly alike. When we do the improbable or impossible together, it's because we have engaged our shared and complementary goodness.

Opening to new kinds of clarity is the ancient art of alchemy, the transmutation of basic materials into gold. Growing together transforms our good and goodness into gold.

Growing together

The new currency of growing together

Growing together is a new conversation in most organizations.

In the old conversations about organizational learning and development, the royal road to team performance was personal development. To this end, leaders would wield the tools of individual performance assessments and performance coaching, performance reviews and performance training mandates.

The operating assumption was the research-unsupported and mechanical metaphor that teams are chains that are only as strong as their weakest links.

As much as this is taken as unquestioned doctrine in slow teams, nimble teams find it quite odd to expect people will move at the tempo of a slowest member.

We now understand teams and organizations from the social and biological metaphors of living networks whose growth is as strong as the sum and synergies of their connections.

When we grow these connections, everyone gets more clarity together.

As individual development helps teams get to certain levels of performance, growing together takes teams to new levels beyond what individual efforts can achieve. When teams are clear that growth is something best done together they become unstoppable.

The science is clear that connected people grow more. Quality connections on nimble teams are not optional. Only with them will we grow together. Our capacity for growing together will always be equal to our capacity for connection.

Connection makes it possible for people to feel valued. People seek new kinds of clarity in their work to the extent they feel valued. Opening to new kinds of connection opens us to new kinds of clarity.

There are three simple ways to grow connections within and between teams that have unique power to support individual and shared growth: shared kindness, being in sync and sense making.

Shared kindness

Kindness is at the heart of connections that make growing together possible. When it is shared, kindness causes trust. Trust is velocity. We move and grow at the speed of trust.

Shared kindness happens through three simple social structures: presence, promises and agreements.

Presence

Presence is being helpful to each other. It is mindful curiosity about what each of us considers helpful at any point in time. This includes categories like assistance, perspectives, ideas, questions, updates, resources and connections.

The presence questions are simple habits, and asked often:

- Do you need help with anything?
- When we are challenged in our work, what would be most helpful to you?

- What are you working on growing and is there anything that would be most useful for me to share?

We can be present to each other when we have capacity constraints, when we have discretionary time in the rhythm of our work, when we encounter any kind of tensions or disconnects and when we want to help each other grow. We help others become present when we ask them for help.

Presence is a performance, connection and growth accelerator. It is based on the humble and realistic realization that it's OK not to know everything and do everything ourselves.

In the vital culture of presence, where we feel free to offer and ask for help whenever it makes sense, we are measurably smarter, faster and better together.

In the weak, slow culture of permission, we are more frustrated and slower together if we lack the freedom to initiate help asks and offers. It's not that we lack capacity for growth, it's that without this freedom, the disconnects keep us from growing together.

Until we grow a culture of presence, we have self-interest, internal toxic competition, fragmentation, disconnects and silos. Freedom to work with presence changes everything.

Promises

Promises are declarations of what we want others to expect from us, how and when. Promises kept strengthen and repair connections.

Promises create emotional freedom in our work. In the Japanese personal growth approach, Morita, when we make a promise, we can keep it no matter how we feel at the time. We act on promise rather than feelings.

We can do it whatever we're feeling. Emotional freedom is knowing we don't have to take responsibility for our feelings, only our actions. We understand they come and go like weather and we can act on promises whatever the internal weather of how we're feeling.

Our capacity for kindness grows when we feel a richer atmosphere of trust from promise making and keeping.

Agreements

Another way to grow a culture of kindness is through agreements. Agreements are shared commitments about how we will work together in specific situations and efforts.

In slow teams, people often work by the tension of assumptions rather than mutually crafted and tested agreements. Tension slows team tempo because it creates disconnects and misalignments.

In nimble teams, we form agreements. We don't assume what will or should happen. Tensions are more rare and temporary. Things happen as we agree they will.

We decide to form agreements on some aspect of our work we want to be smooth and productive. We talk about what matters to everyone in this aspect of work.

Then we craft proposed agreements and make sure we address anything anyone has as a question or concern. We test our best drafted agreements for a period of time, together critique how it went and tweak what we discover into an agreement everyone will share.

We can do this with anything related to communication, organization and interactions. It can even address how non-negotiable standards and regulations will happen. It allows us to collaboratively define what has the power to build and repair trust.

Through presence, promises and agreements, we thrive in cultures of shared kindness. The complements of our goodness allow us to grow into a vibrant, nimble whole more than the sum of our parts.

Being in sync

The churn of uncertainty and ambiguity in any workplace today is dizzying, unpredictable and impossibly managed by any one person.

In nimble teams, we manage the constant of uncertainty and the opportunity of ambiguity by staying in sync. Being in sync is alignment in timing, made possible by freedom in communication and coordination. Sync creates connection. It makes new levels of clarity in our work more possible.

On the communication side of the equation, everyone shares in real time what they know and need, what they're starting and working on, what's changing for them and what they're delivering. People who need any kind of clarification ask for it when they need it.

Coordination sustains alignment among multiple people working on a single deliverable. When things are well coordinated we work from agile and shared understanding of what doneness is for each deliverable, who's working on which parts and how dots need to be connected.

Sync is a challenge in slow teams because the need to work by permission keeps everyone's focus self-centered. Lack of sync in slow cultures is further exacerbated by the slow practices of emails and meetings.

When we're in sync, no balls get dropped. Nothing waits for something else. No one depending on a deliverable wonders about its status or the shared definition of doneness. Handoffs are smooth and optimally timed for momentum toward on time delivery.

Everyone is always on the same agile page, anticipating and responding to any changes that occur along the way.

Teams grow in their capacity for being in sync by growing in the use and mastery of virtual tools, mutual agreements and real time communication and coordination practices.

The commons

In nimble teams, sync thrives in the commons.

The commons is the virtual ecosystem of spaces where everyone can update and get updated, coordinate and collaborate.

We have finally arrived in the arc of technology development where we have tools to support the commons within, between and among teams. Even the simplest virtual spaces we now have make seamless sync possible.

All we need for a commons are three spaces: organized group chat like Slack, workflow organization like Trello and collaborative editing documents like Google. Office 365 and Google + feature versions of all three.

They are easy to use and move teams from slow to nimble when we intersect the technology with the sociology of presence, promises and agreements on how these spaces will be used in everyday work and long view, proactive planning.

They replace the old, slow communication systems and control structures making teams slow and out of sync. These included meetings, reports, emails, document control, performance reviews and personal development plans.

We use the commons to share anything and everything. We share what we're working on, what we're thinking and needing, what we're in progress on and completing, what growing questions we're engaged in and what we're gaining from our work with these questions, the current state of our goodness.

Nimble teams replace email with the commons and get more done through conversations than meetings. In the commons, initiative, inclusion and integrity become continuously possible.

MacroSync

Organizations become more nimble when teams are in sync with each other.

Teams naturally have three kinds of relationships. Some do similar work. Some do work others depend on. Some have specialists who do the same work. Specialists include people in areas like human resources, legal, administrative, technology, marketing, facilities and procurement.

Sync means having regular conversations of presence, promise and agreements. It means everyone keeping their profiles of goodness shared and updated. It means sharing projects seeking common good and requiring shared goodness.

When these teams are not in sync, the whole organization suffers. People become more slow than nimble.

When teams are in sync the whole organization realizes better tempo and responsiveness together. Teams have better capacity to support better tempo and responsiveness. Markets notice and react.

The ambiguity-uncertainty distinction

Being in sync is the most intelligent and effective relationship to life's constant of uncertainty. Nimble teams have as much as slow teams. In fact knowing that growing creates its own kind of uncertainty, nimble teams can actually have more than slow teams.

People in slow teams are characteristically intolerant of uncertainty. They see it as the prime barrier to getting their work done and meeting their numbers. When uncertainty is the enemy, there is little energy left for growth. In fact, the whole idea of creating new abilities makes them anxious in the anticipation that it will just bring about more intolerable uncertainty.

People in nimble teams thrive on uncertainty. That's what allows us to flourish without the illusion of certainty that comes with permissions and approvals. We know no amount of permissions or approvals can reduce the amount of uncertainty we have on any given day.

As a result, we find our power not in a focus on uncertainty but on ambiguity. We realize always being clear is far more realistic and possible than always being certain.

No matter how uncertain we are, we can be clear on our good and goodness.

We can be clear on how we can be helpful to each other. We can be clear on what it means to grow through our work and grow together. Clarity turns uncertainty into a gift to be engaged rather than problem to be fixed.

Getting the future right is not about predicting it right. It's about creating new clarities together. It's about leveraging ambiguity as an asset rather than uncertainty as the enemy.

The 84th problem

As traditional wisdom suggests, nimble teams have 83 problems. 83 is a symbolic number. There are as many challenges and uncertainties in success as failure. They are just different.

The commitment to growing is a commitment to a different set of problems than we now have. One of the juiciest and most realistic questions in any kind of growth focuses on what kinds of problems we dream of having.

Slow teams have 84 problems. The 84th problem is the unrealistic expectation that we will have fewer than 83 problems if we are hard-working, entitled, accountable, capitalized, positioned or smart enough.

How we can make all our problems go away is a slow culture question. It lacks practical value. It is not realistic. There are always 83 problems. Knowing this solves our 84th problem. We become more nimble.

This shifts the problem solving intention from the naive and unproductive search from the problem-free land of unicorns to seeking to have the problems of progress and success we want.

In the land of nimble, we are used to being inventive because we're continuously experimenting with new kinds of value to deliver and new ways to deliver it. Every breakthrough that solves for 5 old problems creates 5 new ones.

When we practice a nimble growth mindset, we think of problems as questions. New questions are golden because progress and growth along any performance metrics moves at the pace that we spark and answer new questions. Growing is all about new questions, the more the merrier.

This illuminates a profound difference between nimble and slow cultures. Slow cultures get stressed and overwhelmed by problems because they don't yet know how to translate these into new questions. Nimble cultures thrive on problems because we always frame these as new questions. We never get bogged down in the insidious 84th problem. We flourish in the iterations and evolutions of all 83.

Unflat: the magic of focus

Slow teams are flat. Their numbers are flat. Their energy is flat. Their brand is flat. Their conversations are flat. Even the games of their mandatory team building events are flat.

Growing together is about getting unflat. Getting unflat is about clarity of focus.

The global study for "The Joy Of Thriving" resulted in the realization that over 90% of the happiest people responding reported that their perspective was the most vital cause of their sense of life meaning and wellbeing. This conclusion mirrors what ancient wisdom traditions and countless current science research studies indicate.

When we're flat, we assume we need a different reality in order to grow together. We see reality as an obstacle rather than asset. When we grow, we don't need a different reality. We understand that we can grow with exactly the reality we have.

Reality is the place where growing occurs. It's a gift, a starting place. In growing we create a new reality not in denial of the reality we have, but because we pay attention to our good and goodness in the reality we have.

This incredibly empowering and liberating understanding forms the fundamental basis of a growing mindset.

We don't live in the victim's hope for a different reality. We don't postpone growing until we feel ready. We don't pretend we can finally grow when we get different work to do, different resources to support us, different leaders to lead us, or even when we can be different ourselves. We grow in the reality we have.

Hoping and pretending reality must first be different keeps us flat.

Getting unflat begins the moment we turn our attention toward work's highest good is creating new abilities together through every opportunity and experience.

Sense making, crazy making

It's curious that on nimble teams, we regularly repeat success and don't repeat mistakes. In slow teams, the opposite happens.

Academic intelligence and work tenure are not necessarily factors in the difference. Nimble teams are not intrinsically higher in IQ or age. What we are better at is making sense of whatever we experience on a daily, weekly, quarterly and annual rhythm.

Sense making is using any planned or unplanned experience to get more clear on what went well, why and what we could do differently next time. It causes us to feel appreciated, creative and optimistic.

The opposite is crazy making. This is using any planned or unplanned experience to examine what went wrong, who's to blame and who's responsible for holding low performers accountable. This causes people to feel self-doubt, unsupported, defensive, counter-blameful, cynical and further risk-averse. History repeats.

Slow teams naively and counterproductively expect that if the weakest people get better, the whole will get better. In nimble teams we know that when we together make sense of our experience, everyone gets better.

Nimble teams reflect on every instance and trend of success and failure with a few simple, powerful sense making questions:

- What went well, planned and unplanned?
- What do we know about why things went well?
- What could we try differently next time?

These beautiful questions make it possible for teams to anticipate and meet future situations with more wisdom, better for making experience their most treasured teacher.

Sense making explains why nimble teams outperform slow teams, even with far more challenges, constraints and uncertainties than slow teams. Our practice of sense making turns every experience into a direct infusion of stronger connections and clarity from experience.

Are nimble people better?

One of the core themes here in the conversation about teams is how culture is not as much a function of individual personalities as it is about the quality of connections and disconnections between and among people on teams.

Nimble teams are nimble because of how they grow together. Slow teams are slow because of how they don't grow together.

What's interesting is how in many slow organizations and teams, we find the nicest, most sincere and dedicated people around. They have to work harder than nimble teams because their culture of business as usual makes everything so much more cumbersome, tedious and slow.

People on slow teams get things done in spite of their culture, precisely because they are so nice, sincere and dedicated.

Many nimble people share similar qualities. They get more done in less time because their priority on growing together gives them coherence and velocity slower teams only dream of, or remember when they worked in more nimble organizations.

Becoming a more nimble team isn't necessarily a call for radical changes in hiring philosophies or priorities. It's about creating the kinds of culture that makes it easy for people to feel valued, connected and free to grow.

Growth is a movement, not a mandate

We can't mandate people to grow. Growing happens when people are inspired into it.

Nothing that matters can be mandated: not passion or commitment, engagement or loyalty, kindness or sync. We will go through the motions in mandates. We only commit to what we trust. We trust what inspires us.

Stories have unique power to inspire us. It's been this way since the beginning of human time. Growth happens and spreads at the rate stories of growth are shared in everyday conversations.

The more we share stories within and across teams of the good we're doing and the goodness making good possible, the more people get inspired for their own and shared growth. Story sharing has an unreasonable power in spreading growth in organizations.

Movements of all kinds are sparked by one credible and contagious story at a time. Storytelling is the media and the message.

The inflection point in the growth of nimble organizations happens when the stories of nimble teams begin to dominate the emotional, social and narrative atmosphere of the organization. When people feel inspired by nimble, they become more nimble.

Realizing our potential

Reality (yes Alice, there still is one)

Being realistic makes us nimble. Nothing slows a team down like having to manage the confusion of unrealistic expectations. Clarity drives the velocity of realistic.

Being realistic has nothing to do with higher powers of prediction about an unknowable future. It is not confusing clarity with plans. It is opening to the clarity that there is always more to reality than we know. Reality is always larger than what we think, feel, experience, believe, assume, understand and expect.

In nimble teams, we never expect we could ever be caught up on or know everything. That might be more possible with the slow of slow teams. Nimble tempo is powered by constant curiosity as much as a slow tempo is powerful by constant need for certainty.

Being realistic is being continuously curious beyond the narrow lens of what we know and assume. It's measuring intelligence in units of honestly posed questions rather than strongly held assumptions. It's knowing we grow in an expansive sense of reality.

This is inspired by the Indian parable of six sightless people discovering an elephant for the first time. One holds an ear, one a leg, one the trunk, one the tail, one a tusk and one a side.

With their own partial information assumed to be complete, they vehemently disagree with everyone else's definition of the whole. They haven't moved from certainty to curiosity that there is a larger reality.

No one, and no collective of even 10 million people, could ever see all of reality at any point in time. All we can do is be curious together about what is beyond the parts of what we see and the assumptions we have about the rest.

Being reality based is the basis of valuing each other and feeling valued. Only with each other can we see more of the whole. We value people we depend on to help us see more. People value us when they depend on us helping them see more of the whole. This is the gift of connection. Being reality based opens us up to new kinds of trusted clarity in every aspect of our craft.

Growing questions

When we ask people on nimble teams what their active growing questions are, they will tell us. They describe what new shifts they would like to make in defining and growing their sense of good and engaging and growing their goodness. They language how we want to be more adaptive and responsive to uncertainty.

Our growing questions are the questions of how to, what if and what would it look like if. Because our world is abundant with uncertainty, we have endless possibilities for new questions. We go into each new day, week and month energized by our growing questions.

People on slow teams don't have growing questions. A culture of permission requires more compliance than opening to new worlds of clarity. Learning is prescribed and assigned.

Without active growing questions, slow work is not an opportunity space for creating new possibilities together. People are left to simply work harder and longer in hope for different results.

Good growing questions have three core qualities:

- They are relevant to the new capabilities and perspectives we want to create in order to empower our work with greater meaning, impact and significance
- They are questions we don't have quick, easy or complete answers to
- They are actionable, given the goodness we already have and the opportunities we have and can create

When crafting good questions, it's useful to interact with experts and people with experience. Through them we discover what we don't know and what we don't know we don't know. This unleashes the possibilities of question based growing.

Every turn on the path of our growth reveals new growing questions. More growing questions lead to better growing questions.

Growing together means working from shared growing questions.

Knowing our potential

Central to any conversations about growth is attention to potential. Slow teams believe their potential is finite and therefore knowable. Nimble teams believe their potentials are unlimited and therefore unknowable.

In slow team cultures, people assume history is destiny. Capabilities equal achievements. It is the fixed mindset of the machine world. If we want to know what a machine is capable of, we look at its performance history. We test machines to predict future capabilities.

Before current science research, people assumed certain personalities and age groups were more or less capable of developing new capabilities. The message was perhaps unnerving yet nonetheless guilt-relieving and time-saving: You can't change people. You can't teach old dogs new tricks.

The studies of neuroplasticity in the neurosciences now make it clear that our brains have unlimited development potential. There are no permanent structures in the brain. Every instance of creating new abilities and clarity restructures the brain.

We can learn how to do anything others do that we can physically do. There is no evidence to support limits, except what's physically impossible to do. The only limits otherwise are about readiness. When we're ready to grow, we do. When we're not, we don't. Even when we're not ready, we are still capable.

Even with old dogs. Research now indicates that old dogs can take longer to learn new tricks, but they do. More importantly, they show stronger skill application abilities than younger dogs.

The realistic expectation is that we can't know anyone's potential. All we can do is liberate them from a fixed mindset by cultivating and engaging growth mindsets.

For most of us, personality assessments tell us what dispositional boxes we operate in. With a "This is who you are" expert diagnosis of our potential, these tests intentionally or unintentionally reinforce a fixed mindset.

Many people have gone through most of the more common tests that challenge them to make sense of the bizarre conclusion they are an "extrovert-thinking, water-centric, type 5, green, woo driver."

It is an incredible and unrealistic constraint to think one or a few prescribed labels, in language not our own, could describe the boundaries of our potential.

Intended or not, we don't hear someone read their personality test tea leaves and go on about all the new ways they want to grow and blossom beyond their diagnosis. The diagnosis feels more like a prognosis. People feel more disconnected from their potential, and from each other.

We know more of our potential by opening up to new kinds of clarity about any aspects of our work and world. In work as continuous discovery and exploration we discover more of our unlimited potential.

Knowing our brains have no limits makes us ready to grow.

The power of readiness

It's one thing to commit to growth. It's another to actually grow. We create grow when we're ready to. No amount of internal urgency or external pressure has the power to substitute for growth readiness.

Readiness is the intersection of optimism and freedom. Optimism is believing we have the basics required to grow. Freedom is the feeling we're choosing to grow, for whatever reasons we have.

We won't even begin growing if we feel pessimism or pressure. This is why in slow teams, unreadiness for growth sustains business as usual.

The most effective way to shut down readiness in others is to get people focused on their weaknesses, failures and gaps and follow up with a mandate that they getting better in ways we prescribe. These kill the optimism and freedom of readiness.

Remembering all the important shifts and evolutions in our life energizes optimism. Having ever-evolving growing questions energizes freedom. The nimble feel freedom to grow their craft together.

One of the most significant constraints on growing readiness is identity. If we don't see ourselves as someone who can do something even adequately, we won't even attempt to develop it.

Each of us has examples of people we admire for their amazing abilities and accomplishments that we feel confident are far beyond our potentials.

The more we see them as different from us, the more we believe we lack the ingredient abilities and qualities to achieve what they do. We feel clear that we are simply not the kinds of people they are.

We usually don't realize how much more we can grow until the steady progress of our growth reveals how we have what it takes to grow beyond our doubts. Evidence of readiness is that we're actively engaged in new vistas of clarity about what we can make possible in our world.

Self-improvement and growth

The good news on growth is that we don't have to change who we are to grow. We always have what it takes for the next steps in our growth.

Every time we have grown in our lives, it was from exactly who we were at the time. We engaged the good, goodness, and connections we had. We didn't have to first become someone else. Who we were shifted, not for the change but from it.

New levels of clarity come from new questions, perspectives and connections. Each of us has what these require. We have more goodness than we will ever need to realize the good we seek together.

What gives us this kind of resident potential is how we can combine our goodness in new ways. If we live or grow from just eight of our abilities and qualities we had by the time we were 12, there are 40,320 kinds of combinations of goodness possible.

When we grow, we grow from this immense potential.

Talking with people at high levels of mastery in their fields reveals that the more clarity they have on their goodness the more passion they have in their craft. They don't think being better is prerequisite to growing even more.

Getting better is possible in growth but it isn't the core consciousness of growing. In slow cultures, the getting better mindset is a thinly veiled version of a deficiency perspective. Greater clarity is the heart of growing. It is living and working in oneness to wonder.

The learning conversation

In nimble organizations, the conversation is about growing together. Learning happens naturally when our focus is growing together. Growing is a richer lens for developing capacity for connection and efficacy.

In slow organizations, the conversation is not about growth. It's about learning as removing weaknesses for better attitude, performance and loyalty.

An irony is how people in slow organizations never know where they're going to find time for learning. People in nimble organizations would never think they have to find time for growing together. It happens in the flow of everyday work.

In slow cultures everyone is reminded, at least annually, how no one is ever good enough. Denial of such is somewhere between blasphemy and treason.

The narrative is that if everyone would become more of who they aren't, everything would get better for everyone. Goals would be met.

At this point globally, companies are annually spending over $300 billion on training and to show for it they are still getting over 80% employee and leadership disengagement. Goals are not being met. That's the state of weakness remediation.

The slow culture prescription for getting better is knowing more. People are sent to workshops and webinars to consume more knowledge. Success is measured in checked boxes of attendance, passed quizzes and cashing in on performance review improvements.

People with higher level degrees and specializations are entitled to higher levels of respect and deference.

An amazing amount of time is spent getting people up to date so they know as much as possible what's going on in the business. There is no evidence that the massive and expensive amounts of updates add up to people growing more.

The needle moves when the conversation shifts to growing. It begins with the blinding flash of the obvious that knowing more is not necessarily more clarity in work. Clarity has its own distinct integrity in how we grow together.

The confusion factor

The opposite of clarity is confusion. Confusion is not lack of knowing. It's not having more questions than answers, more knowns than unknowns. Knowing more doesn't necessarily create new kinds of clarity. Clarity is about wondering more.

What's fascinating about confusion is that it's very possible to not know we're in it. Research indicates that most people who are confused have no way of knowing they are, because other trusted confused people keep confirming their confused beliefs.

Confusion is mistaking assumption for reality. It's working from what we believe to be true rather than what is. The only way to stay confused is to have no new questions. The only way to not know we're confused is to have no new questions.

When slow organizations equate knowing and improving, they make it more uncomfortable for people to work from their questions because in slow cultures, questions are instant signs of weakness. The weak are a species at risk.

Confusion keeps slow teams slow. It causes people to be awkward, risk-averse and cautious. It diminishes capacity for traction and tempo.

In slow teams, the opportunities for confusion are endless. People assume what they do and don't have approval for. They assume when they will and won't garner forgiveness and looking the other way by the owners of consequences.

People assume the power they do and don't have. They assume what others think of them, need, want and have to share. People assume how much they're satisfying and disappointing others. They assume they know why the team's tempo is compromised by waiting and rushing.

Every instance of confusion is somewhere between a speed bump and a sacred cow in the road.

On nimble teams, everyone's clarity questions feel welcomed and valued. Moments of confusion are more rare and we have our nimble tempo and endless growing to show for it.

Nimble leaders are clear that people grow in greater openness to new kinds of clarity. They help everyone feel loved for their new questions.

Inspiring clarity

It only takes one inspiring reason to create new clarity. Among the many, there are three simple intentions: impact, fluency and mindfulness.

The Impact intention

We want new kinds of clarity to bring about more benefits to ourselves, others or both. We believe it will make a greater good possible, or good for more possible. The further out in time we go to define the good we seek, the more impact intention we have for growing in our work.

The Fluency intention

We want more fluency in something, doing it more easily, or efficiently. We want to be less self-conscious and unsure about it. We want to struggle less with it. We want to do it with more confidence. Fluency is evident in things needing less time and effort.

The Mindfulness intention

We want to do something with more variations, to make it more interesting, engaging or enjoyable.

Mindfulness means doing something, even a habit, differently each time. The variations can be micro level, very small. Mindfulness brings a freshness and creativity which is useful when it's important to adapt to the nuances of different situations.

Any combination of these intentions gives us more energy, endurance and persistence in any growth curve. Every successful effort to create new abilities brings with it new problems, challenges and the questions we translate these into.

Inspiring reasons don't include extrinsic threats, bribes and lectures. These have no power to get or keep us growing. They diminish growth readiness. Growth needs its own reasons to thrive beyond the effort required and uncertainties implied.

Speaking of weaknesses

Removing weaknesses is a reason to grow, but not one of the three that have inspiration and sustainability power.

Weakness connotes something we do that disappoints the expectations of others or our own. Weaknesses often fall in the categories of what might be unhelpful to others or ourselves.

Calling something a weakness doesn't make growing together more likely or easier. Weakness is an assessment, not one of the levels of potential, just as weed is an assessment, not one of the 400,000 known plant species.

The act of naming things we do weaknesses has no power to bring about clarity. Judging ourselves doesn't factor into this process.

We can think of a weakness as an ability that gets in the way of some form of good we seek. We can have the weakness of procrastination, unhealthy eating or being disorganized. Each is a developed ability or quality. The only way we can lose an ability is to lose the physical capacity required or to somehow forget how to do it. This why it's possible to have lifelong weaknesses.

Reality is, when we reflect back on all the good we have done and created in our lives and work, they all happened while we had all kinds of weaknesses.

The nimble irony of weaknesses is that if we have some new ability or quality we want to develop, and the development of any new ability or quality intrinsically means not doing it well until we do, and a weaknesses is something we don't do well, a commitment to growing is a commitment to having new weaknesses. Nimble teams get this.

This is an incomprehensible logic to people on slow teams who work in dread of being caught having weaknesses, as the costs and risks of having them are completely intolerable. To resist new weaknesses prevents growth that stagnates performance, that brings about even greater risks and costs. And no growth.

The reality of self-assessment

Growing is impacting our world with new forms of good. We can know some of our impact. The rest is known by others who see what we can't.

This is the limitation of self-assessment. Only with the perspectives of others can we accurately assess whether and to what degree we're creating good that benefits others as they define benefit.

We grow to the extent we stay curious about what others know about our impact that we don't, and cant.

It's always being curious about perspective differences. One person's likes are another's dislikes. The opposite of curiosity is assuming the first or loudest person giving us perspectives represents everyone else.

In curiosity, we seek a variety of perspectives. We also don't settle for judgments. We don't get caught up in assumption-abundant, adolescent assessments of terrific and terrible.

We use our growing questions to glean useful and actionable details. Above all we certainly don't assume our self-assessment is an accurate or complete picture of how well we're growing.

The F word

One of the prime nutrients for any kind of growing is the gift of perspective from others.

Useful perspective comes in the form of ideas, options, stories, new questions and asks related to future use contexts.

When we ask for or offer perspective, we can do so without references to the notorious "F word" of feedback. We don't have to go around announcing that we have some "feedback" for people not asking for it.

Feedback for many is an emotionally charged word. It doesn't usually signal oncoming kindness, compassion and helpfulness. It often signals oncoming criticizing, blaming, bullying, lecturing or demeaning. It provokes self-protection and defensiveness. It doesn't matter that it is motivated by catharsis, confession or conversion. It shuts down readiness for growth.

We can more simply, and helpfully, talk about offering and asking for the kindness of each other's "perspective." It feels more friendly and frankly grows more mutual trust. Growth thrives in a culture of trust. Trust thrives in the anticipation of and delivery of kindness.

Perspective conversations are more simple, less drama and trauma. We don't have to put trust at risk by going on about past complaints and grievances. We don't have to walk around on eggshells trying to avoid adult conversations.

We don't have to waste time arguing with others about our innocence. We don't have to compromise our sense of agency with declarations of our victimhood.

All we need to do is, in a palpable attitude of kindness, offer and share useful ideas, options, stories, good questions and asks related to future opportunities and contexts.

The emphasis on future makes it kind. In perspective conversations, people feel cared for, understood, supported, curious, connected, inspired, optimistic and ready to grow.

The magic of receptivity

We are most receptive to perspectives we ask for. It is unrealistic to think anyone will be receptive to what they didn't ask for or invite, no matter how brilliant or helpful we think we are. We support what we welcome.

There are four parts to these conversations.

We start by sharing with others what we are working on. Then we share what we would most like perspective on, when, how and why. We ask others if there other kinds of perspectives they have and are willing to share as well. Finally, we ask if there are any perspectives they would find helpful from us relative to new things they're working on growing.

This conversation makes mutual perspective sharing welcome and optimizes receptivity and mutual trust. It prevents the tension of uncertainty around whether our ideas will be received in trust or rejected in tension.

The key is to have the conversation regularly. We don't have to try assuming whether others are working on something, if they want our support with anything or if they have perspectives we didn't even know to ask for. We can be regularly and mutually clear. We can be welcomed and useful sources of shared growth support.

Abandoning performance reviews: It's time

Useful perspectives happen quickly, ideally in real time while they're still actionable. When we care about people, we don't even postpone them a week much less a year. Withholding perspective is a core barrier to growth and trust. It is passive aggressive behavior, not useful kindness and support.

We would drop any friends in a minute who one day say they have perspective for us but they're keeping it secret until an annual performance review they'll ambush us with. Or worse, they will instead go around and collect anonymous feedback from our peers and deliver it to us. What could possibly be more toxic and growth diminishing?

This is why we need to design quick perspective and perspective welcoming loops into all dimensions of work so people can be nimble in their growth and course-correct as soon as possible.

And while we're at it, let's rethink roles

While we're abandoning performance reviews let's rethink the growth implications of roles.

For planned and unplanned tasks that emerge in our work, who does what is typically determined by four classic assignment habits: leader assignment, historical norms, defined roles and shared initiative.

Leader assignment can be based on any combination of individual capability assessment, availability assumptions, job description interpretations, personality dynamics, teams politics and self-interest.

Historical norms address who has typically done what in the past. This might or might not relate to actual capabilities, opportunities, availabilities, job descriptions or politics. People do what they've always done.

Defined roles are formal, approve task specific rules and job descriptions about who has permission to do and not do what.

These three habits are common in slow teams. They contribute to slow tempo and inhibit growth because people don't feel free to initiate their growth or help others grow beyond the boundaries of these assignment habits.

Shared initiative is the norm in nimble teams. Six simple things happen. People see what needs to be done, check if anyone else is working on it, decide if they can do it, let others know they're on it, ask for help if they need, and get it done. This is working from clarity rather than confusion, sync rather than supposition.

Nothing waits for permissions. Nothing slips through the cracks of approved assignments. The ten thousand things a day that cannot possibly be planned, predicted or anticipated get handled easily. Best of all, with this freedom for initiative, people can take on what would help them grow

People take on work through presence, promise and agreements. Each of these happen in the rhythm of conversations multiple times a day, week month and quarter. As a result, people can take on work in ways that helps them move along the potential continuum from fixed to growth mindset.

In a culture of shared initiative, people grow through work pairing and rotating. People pair with others to teach and develop new forms of goodness. People rotate work in order to grow and strengthen new forms of goodness.

When people grow together, they have the freedom to do what they can that needs to be done. When people are slow together, they see something that they can do and needs to be done and ignore it, losing a potential growth opportunity.

Optimal growth happens when people have minimal role restrictions that allow for them to work in sync together.

Should we expect people to do their jobs?

There is a specious logic in expecting if people are hired to do a job, they should do it.

The major flaw in this logic is the assumption that hiring managers and candidates could predict what this job will encounter in the future. Jobs can change beyond the originals competencies required and hired.

It might be more realistic to expect that work will change in ways that people might or might not be prepared for.

One implication is that in a world of change, uncertainty and ambiguity, the most important ability to assess for in hiring or promoting any candidate is the ability to grow.

Do they have a growing mindset? Do they see how this work could be an optimal context for their growth? What curiosity do they bring to this work? What would they want to discover? What would they want to experiment with? What makes them feel most support in growing? What does it mean to them to grow with others? What new abilities are they ready to create?

We cannot realistically expect people to do their job in work where change is a constant, unless they come into it with dedication to growing. We can expect people dedicated to growing to do the work.

Flawless failure

One of the ways to know a team is slow is to talk with people about their relationship to mistakes. For all manner of reasons, people in slow teams will do anything to stay out of trouble.

One efficient way to avoid mistakes is to try nothing new. This is flawless failure to grow. To seek a life of avoiding mistakes is to seek a life without growth, discovery or awe.

The tradeoff is simple. Trying nothing new, we get to live without a sense of mistake making and failure, at the cost of gaining no new growth. We trade innocence for growth. Everything is slow. Flat stays flat.

Nimble people have a different relationship to mistakes. We value how new mistakes are signs we're doing some vital experimenting.

It's interesting talking with nimble people growing together. We have much to say when asked about what we're trying new. We have story portfolios brimming with examples of works in progress, things done right the second or fifth or twentieth time, lessons from progressively fewer mistakes and faster failures to more successes. We are clear growth declines in the naive commitment to doing new things right the first time.

We work with the fearless and shameless messy business of creating new kinds of clarity. When our performance is stellar it's not because we're obsessed with flawless performance but because we're focused on new kinds of clarity.

The nimble can relate to so many of the world celebrated studio artists who gladly report the biggest thing in their vibrantly innovative spaces is their dumpster.

Good and goals

Nimble teams are inspired by good. Slow teams are perspired by goals.

Good is a lens. Creating the future from a lens of good is perfect in a world of change and uncertainties. Good is not a prediction. It is not a set of assumptions about an intrinsically unknowable future.

As an inspiring lens, our sense of good reveals new possibilities in the present. We can adapt it to whatever happens unplanned. We are continuously making progress toward the future we want to see possible. In the world of good, success is progress toward good. We cannot predict our way into the future, but we can create it through inspiration and progress.

Progress toward good energizes us and catalyzes our growth together. As our world shifts, our sense of good shifts into new lenses of inspiration.

Goals are locations. They are predicted assumptions about a future that has no intrinsic commitment to predictability. They don't shift as reality shifts. We either succeed or fail in achieving them, based on how accurate or inaccurate our predicted assumptions were.

With intolerance of uncertainty, the first reaction people in slow teams have to approved goals is doubt in their ability to pull them off. They are not comforted by predictive assumptions in an unpredictable world. After unsuccessfully negotiating for goal downgrades to the level of their self-doubt, they get busy working on their excuses.

Their self-doubt makes them even more awkward, risk-averse and cautious, leading to the disproportionate amount of goal fail we see in organizations. When their definition of success needs to match their current level of low self-confidence, goals swim at the shallow end of the inspiration pool.

As assumptions, goals become unrealistic at the rate we pursue them. Goal achievement is more rare and there is little data supporting that it is definitively related to happiness at work.

The failure rate of performance, change management and strategic goals in organizations is over 80%. When people feel like they're failing over 80% of the time, they work with lower levels of intrinsic motivation and performance. They will endure going through the motions of setting and taking on goals with as much faith in them as they have in themselves and each other.

In nimble teams, our 3-part recipe for nimble is deciding what's good, getting busy making progress towards it and updating our definition of good as we progress our way into the future we want to see and create.

Because all of our work is question based, our sense of good is often more detailed and researched than goals. In slow cultures, people tend to aim low to avoid failure or aim vaguely enough to support the appearance of success.

Because realistic is not a requirement for the lens of the good we seek, our sense of good is regularly more aspirational than goals. That's why they have unique aspirational power.

Some of the most amazingly transformative things around today came about not because realistic and approved goals were in place but because people progressed their way into the most beautiful and agile good they made possible.

Gratefully, teams of scientists this year will commit to progress on the improbable good of curing and preventing the spectrum of childhood cancers. If they never get to a predicted point in an optimistic timeframe but create amazing breakthroughs in the meantime, everyone gains. All that matters is how they declare and make progress toward the beautiful good they most seek.

Good and great things happen because we work from five powerfully inspiring, organizing and engaging clarity questions.

- What's the good we want to ultimately see and what would represent progress towards that?
- What do we need to research, decide, clarify and confirm for this progress to be possible?
- What abilities can we engage and grow to support this progress?
- How does our sense of good need to shift based on our experience and progress going forward?

These questions keep us focused, aligned, agile and productive. Exceeding what would have been a finite, non-adaptive and assumptive goal is possible with inspiration without limits and progress without end.

Progress is everything

Harvard researchers indicate that recognition of progress rather than success is most related to meaningful and engaging work. As much as we hope goals inspire us, every day we don't reach our goals, we feel like we are failing. Progress is different. Progress is possible every day.

The interesting dynamic in progress is that each step often requires a different kind of clarity.

When we're 30% of the way toward some kind of a clearly defined good we seek, what matters is being clear together on what the progress of 35% looks like.

We can be clear on what 65% will look like when we get to 60%. The math of this implies that when we're just starting out toward realizing any clear and inspiring good, we can have no idea what success at 100% will look like. Each step of progress reveals what the next step of progress will look like. 100% will be clear when we reach progress at 95%.

The power of a clearly defined, inspiring sense of good is its ability to reveal new possibilities for progress at each point along the way. Because our desired good is a lens rather than location, this lens can shift with every next step in progress gained and how the world shifts and changes along the way.

In profound contrast to every day feeling drained and deficient by failing to meet our goals, each experience of progress creates new levels of energy, alignment and growth. This is the power of clarity.

When the nimble start up a mountain to the good we ultimately seek, every mindful turn in the path reveals other unpredictable paths and richer versions of good.

We stay curious of the possibilities our goals could never predict. We dream and walk together in wondrous clarity of letting the mountain tell us the best ways to get to the good we seek.

Progress (In)tolerance

In nimble cultures where progress is our priority, our work is alive and growth rich in continuous experimenting. When we're uncertain something interesting and promising will give us the progress we seek, we try it out. We make reality our most wise and trusted guide to the good we seek.

In slow cultures where people have no tolerance for uncertainty, they talk things do death. The need for approval prevents the possibilities for clarity. No matter how much lip service they give to change and innovation, slow organizations are learning disabled precisely because of their intolerance of uncertainty.

Interestingly, there is as much uncertainty in trying something new as there are uncertainties unleashed by approvals. Approvals only create the illusion of certainty.

We can look back at every instance of approval and see that as many uncertainties followed as would have been experienced in several iterations of trying new things. If experimenting is accelerated growing, approvals are postponed learning.

When the dominant, most vocal people in slow organizations show a persistent intolerance for progress in a bias for perfection, growth shuts down, or moves quietly to the margins. In obsession with certainty, thinly veiled as addiction to being right, approval occurs when the last question leaves the room.

In the absurd pledge of allegiance to zero mistakes, they postpone growing together. They fail slower.

Learning disabled organizations are easy to assess for. All we have to do is to go around counting the numbers of meetings, meetings before and after meetings, endless reports, approval layers, lip service paid to accountability and unhealthy life-work relationships.

In a nimble world, we see everything as an experiment. Everything, even things decided by others, is a fresh opportunity for growing in progress, not an excuse for growth diminishing perfection.

We find out what works by piloting it out, often with early adopters who are always antsy for something other than business as usual. They help us grow good into better because they prefer quick progress over slow perfection.

It's easy to assess for nimble cultures. Everyone is always engaging their goodness in experiments of one kind or another. Early adopters feel loved. Innovators feel valued. Our markets feel rewarding.

The primacy of habits

There is interesting emerging evidence that we can bring about new kinds of good simply by growing and engaging habits that make them possible. Habits are things we do automatically.

Being nimble can be a matter of defining the good we seek, deciding what kinds of habits would support progress and then growing these habits. Habits make progress toward good possible.

People grow into good writers and athletes, artists and programmers simply by the daily habits they cultivate. Even without finite and time stamped goals, they exceed even their own hopes. Each of us regularly does well because of the habits that support us doing well. This the power of habit.

Habits are living things. We grow them through action.

With science based research on habits, we now understand that they are not the result of will power, skills training, mandates, incentives or role clarity.

Will power is variable and so not dependable enough to help with habit consistency. Will power fluctuates with our moods, health, fatigue, levels of uncertainty and ambiguity and situational factors.

Skills training, no matter how expensive, entertaining, change championed or repeated result in skills. Skills are optional abilities. Habits are not. They are automatic, not just optional. It takes habit building beyond skills training to build durable habits.

Mandates and incentives seem like logical strategies. As boisterous and seductive they might be, they lack the power to build habits. No one can build a habit for someone else. Everyone has to do their own work. Mandates can give us reasons to grow habits but that's all they contribute. Reasons are necessary but insufficient conditions.

Knowing our roles in even the most precise detail doesn't substitute for the growing and sustainability of habits. Role clarity can tell us which habits we are committing to, but developing them takes far more than this assumption.

Building new habits

Now that we have the science and research of habits, championed by people like Charles Duhigg, intentional habit growing is now possible.

New habits result from knowing our reasons, giving it time, progressing in steps and practicing mindfully.

Knowing our reasons

The more clear we become on the potential benefits of a new habit, the more energy we have for growing it. The more reasons we have for a habit, the more energy we have to persist and endure beyond good intentions and will power.

Giving it time

Habits grow when we decide when, in exactly what situations and what conditions, we will practice the new habit. Optimal timing to grow and strengthen a new habit is just before or after an existing habit we enjoy or find important.

Progressing in steps

We start small, in micro actions. We do the simplest version of the habit. We do it on a frequency that is achievable for us. Then we increase the duration and frequency of the habit, one step at a time. We use the momentum of progress to move us forward.

Practicing mindfully

This is practicing habits with slight variations in how and we do them. This makes them more interesting, more rewarding and therefore stronger and more durable.

How habits become persistent

Neuroscience now reveals that when we start to practice new habits, two things are released: biologically, the feel-good reward chemical dopamine and psychologically, a sense of certainty.

In a double-loop reinforcing spiral, dopamine and certainty release each other and strengthen the growth of new habits. This dynamic is multiplied by having meaningful reasons for any new habit we create.

When we are not particularly stressed, our brain has a bias for new habits, activating them more quickly than old habits. When we're stressed, our brain defaults to old habits. And so the vital importance of sustaining a sense of presence in any ways we can, including mindfulness practices.

The good news here is that old habits never die, they just become irrelevant as our brain prefers new habits. All we need is to grow the habits we want

What to do with old habits

We all have old habits that, even though they might have served is well in the past, do not serve our good or progress now.

No matter how motivated we are to get rid of old habits, our brain is hardwired to choose them until we grow viable habit alternatives. They persist in the absence of new growing habits.

Getting rid of bad habits is not a function of commitment and will power. It's a matter of growing new replacement habits.

Old habits become irrelevant in the growth of new habits options. Our brain gives preference to new habits as we make them stronger with practice and mindfulness. This is how our old habits originally began and grew.

We don't have to understand why old habits started in the first place. We don't have to launch campaigns against them. All we have to do is grow new habits.

Mindless systems and processes

In most slow organizations serious about command and control, efficiency is King. Amazing amount of things can be justified in the name efficiency. Anything but the bottom line can be sacrificed.

The usual targets of efficiency are systems and processes. Nimble teams don't worry much about efficiency because we are already nimble. Always creating new levels of clarity makes us faster together. Always growing from experience, we accelerate new levels of performance all the time.

In slow cultures where the permission-based obsession with efficiency slows things down, the approach is making systems and processes as mindless as possible. By removing variations in them, people lose their ability to notice and respond quickly to variations. This is the definition of being mindless. Mindless people struggle with tempo.

In nimble cultures, we work with mindfulness. We are continuously being conscious of and responsive to changes and shifts in our work and world. Efficiency is not a matter of cost cutting. It's a matter of growing into more mindful human beings and teams in all we do.

Taking charge of our habit landscape

One of the most intelligent ways to make sense of habit growth is to map out the habits that shape the landscape of our work and life.

Habits live along a continuum between strong and emerging. Strong habits are habits we do well and consistently. The more we practice a habit, the more automatic it is, the less we need motivation or will power for them. We just do them without first having to decide to. Emerging habits are those we're just developing through practice. They are not yet done well and consistently.

Habits also live along a continuum between useful and not-useful. Useful habits are habits aligned with our good. They make our lives and work easier, more enjoyable and successful. Not-useful habits are not aligned with our good. If we have a passion for well-being, habits of bad nutrition and excessive sitting are not useful habits.

There are specific strategies for each matrix quadrant.

Strong/Useful

We can learn how to develop more mastery of these habits by learning from people who are better at them than we. We can become more mindful in how we do them. We can become more aware of how they align with our good.

Strong/Emerging

We can make these more automatic by pairing them with existing strong habits, whether they're more or less useful. Pairing happens when we do an emerging habit just before or after a strong habit. We can become more aware of how they align with our good. We can learn how to do them more skillfully.

Not-useful/Emerging

We can weaken these even further by making them less convenient to do. If we have an emerging habit of eating certain foods that are not aligned with our passion for good nutrition, we can make sure we don't bring them into our house in the first place. If we want to be less tempted to text and drive, we leave our phones in the trunk while driving.

Not-useful/Strong

We reduce and remove non-useful-strong habits by building and scheduling useful habits to replace them. Instead of spending too much time on social media, we create a new habit of taking a walk or doing some yoga the instant we feel sucked into a vortex of social mind numbness.

We can intentionally shape our habit landscape. Our brains have no intrinsic interest in or attachment to any habits. We can grow and replace any habits we want. We can grow more beauty in our world from a rich and dynamic habit ecosystem.

Engagement

Why Google And Apple Outperform

The performance difference in admired companies is engagement.

According to Bain research, companies like Apple, Netflix and Google are 40% more productive than the average company.

They prefer strong cultures to strong people. These nimble companies have 16% star players, while other companies have 15%. With similar mix of star players, they produce substantially more output. They invest in high engagement cultures.

They prefer engaged and inspired to merely satisfied people. An engaged employee is 44% more productive than a satisfied worker, but an employee who feels inspired at work is nearly 125% more productive than a satisfied one. Companies that inspire more employees perform better than the rest.

That's the power of working from a lens of good and goodness. That's the power of nimble.

The engagement difference

Engagement and satisfaction are distinctly different phenomena. If we're measuring for satisfaction, we're not measuring for engagement.

Satisfaction is about people as consumers rather than contributors. It's about how well people think leaders are doing for them. Investments in satisfaction can paradoxically lead to steady declines in engagement. Engagement is about people as contributors.

Satisfaction is about the seductive addiction to extrinsic rewards. Extrinsic rewards trigger the reward chemicals of dopamine in the brain. The more dopamine we experience, the more we need just to stay satisfied.

This is why no matter what we give people in extrinsic satisfaction, the more they require and demand. The more inconsolable they feel. It's a no-win proposition. The organization and everyone loses.

Enduring joy is only possible with the intrinsic rewards of engagement. Engagement is the degree to which people co-create their work together with a sense of feeling values, connected and free to grow.

Engaged people together define how work works. They decide together how communication and decision making, planning and alignment, sync and workflow happen. They share authorship of their growing and their work. People engage in what they help create.

Assessing for engagement means discovering where people feel free to do their best, organize themselves, get useful perspectives and grow. It's exploring how connected they feel to each other and those who depend on the value they produce. It's determining how much time they spend doing what matters to them, what lights them up and what they most want to see possible and grow.

The culture question

These days, talk about organizational culture dominates board room and C Suite conversations. There is a sense that culture is the make or break factor in performance and growth, differently significant compared to strategy and structure. It seems as important as it is elusive.

Culture is how people engage with each other on a daily basis. It is not the espoused priorities of a centralized planning committee, the behavioral mandates from the top or the policies, procedures and protocols of accountability departments.

Culture cannot be announced, planned, controlled, managed or engineered. These are functions of machines. Culture is organic. It can only be grown within and between teams, by people within and between teams.

Culture grows as people get better at knowing their goodness and engaging it to create the good they seek together. It is their relationship to clarity.

Culture is the core source of how it feels to work together and the prime shaper of how much we grow together. Every organization and each team in it has its own signature feeling. It's palpable when you walk in, see how quickly or slowly things happen and listen to the energy of the workbuzz.

How long does it take for people to grow together?

Growth is not a goal. There is no end point from which to move onto something else. Growth is not a check box. It is not something anyone can take credit or blame for. Growing is a journey with its own path toward increasingly realizing our potentials.

The question of how long it takes for people to grow is an old question, and so not a useful one. People grow individually and together in their own way, at their own rate. Growing happens in unpredictable and iterative steps and phases. We accelerate it by making it the point of work.

Most leaders unconsciously slow growth. They haven't learned how they contribute to growth speed bumps. This dynamic is exacerbated by their unrealistic expectation that slowness is caused by the incompetencies of their teams or bosses.

Nimble leaders know exactly how growth in people and teams works. They have grown clarity on what they can contribute as catalysts, coaches and connectors to accelerate growth in all its forms.

The power of momentum

Accelerating our growth into more nimble teams is not about drama.

We don't have to launch extensive and expensive campaigns. We don't have to pull people away from work for big speeches and lofty pontifications. We don't have to flaunt the latest in management fashions down the runways of slide decks. We don't have to run big goals up slippery flagpoles. These engage no one.

We don't have to make engagement mysterious. On any given day, engagement means keeping momentum on progress. The tempo of nimble teams is the function of momentum.

When growth is our most beautiful priority at work, all we need is momentum toward progress in what we together author as good. Momentum is the optimal media for engagement.

With clarity on the good we seek, there are several ways we build and sustain momentum.

Beginning in curiosity

Momentum often begins in uncertainty. When we make lists of all our unknowns and knowns, the unknowns list is longer. We instantly spark momentum when we identify the questions we will be working from. We don't ever have to wait for certainty. All we have to do is move toward clarity one good question at a time.

Chucking things down

We gain momentum when we break down large efforts into the logical sequence of their parts and work in order on one part at a time. This is particularly realistic when we only get small chunks of time for anything on any given day. Each step supports the building and sustaining of momentum. In a nimble culture of momentum, our work doesn't take energy. It creates it.

Practicing a bias for incomplete progress

Nimble people love incomplete progress. We don't measure success in units of instant satisfaction. Work in progress is our badge of nimble. We know every day of delightful success is preceded by a thousand days of satisfying, incomplete progress.

Keeping a good rhythm of steps

Nimble teams know momentum is about rhythm. Rhythm is the regular pulse of action in any effort. It's doing a little each day on anything rather than a lot less frequently. It's organizing ourselves in two week cadences of sprints. This keep continuity of energy. People in slow teams leave gaps between actions large enough to lose energy and then need to start momentum all over again. The nimble work in brisk and even rhythms.

Being resilient

In nimble cultures, we do not take personally changes we don't cause. If change causes us to reshape our sense of what's good, we adapt as quickly and seamlessly as possible. If our resources or constraints change, we fluidly adjust what progress and momentum means.

Momentum doesn't take courage and energy. It creates them. We work with fewer excuses, postponements, fear and regrets. Every possibility becomes a gift. Momentum is the mother of all realized dreams.

What's the rush?

It's fascinating to observe the tempo of teams.

Because they don't work in sync to create and sustain momentum, slow teams work in a bipolar tempo of waiting and rushing.

They wait for approvals and permissions. They wait for other people to get things done who wait for approvals and permissions to get things done. They wait to feel motivated. They wait for focus, decisions and priorities. They wait until they feel enough trust.

Waiting is the egg to the chicken of rushing. It's one of work's juiciest ironies that people on slow teams rush around more than nimble teams do. In a culture of momentum, there is minimum waiting and rushing. There is steady progress.

When people feel free to take initiative, include others in what they're up to and work with integrity, nothing is postponed in waiting. Nothing is compromised in rushing. Tempo creates beauty in work.

Smarter together

When we grow together we stay engaged through initiative, inclusion and integrity. They make us better and faster together. They give growth meaning and velocity.

Initiative is seeing what needs to be done, checking in with others to see if anyone is already working on it and doing whatever we can to move things forward. It's not waiting, hoping, assuming or needing permissions. It's not avoiding things we don't think is our "our job."

In nimble teams, job descriptions read the same: When you see something that needs to be done, do it. The endless costs of reengineering work processes and systems would be unnecessary in nimble cultures of initiative taking.

Inclusion is working in sync with others on whatever needs to be done. It's deciding together, not assuming, who's going to do what and when. It's sharing work tasks to give them more velocity or to help someone get better at something by working with someone who's better at it. It's the power of twos.

Integrity is dependability. It's the transparency of letting people know what we're up to at any point in time. It's working with presence, promises and agreements rather than assumptions, tensions and disconnects.

What motivates us

One of the differences between nimble and slow performers is their motivation. It's not that the nimble have motivation and the slow lack it. Everyone is motivated. The difference is in the kind of motivation. The nimble work with internal motivation. The slow work with external motivation.

The nimble work from the good they seek. They are intrinsically motivated by dedication to their growth and the growth of their teams. They are naturally energized by feeling valued, connected and free to make progress toward good.

Making a positive difference infuses their work with intrinsic meaning. They are not motivated by imposed bribes or threats. They are insulted by them. Their motivation is transformational.

Motivation for the slow is transactional. The slow work for what they have permission to do. They work for whatever pay, position and protection they feel they earn by the permissions they satisfy. When work lacks intrinsic meaning, it must be compensated by surrogate satisfiers.

When we reinvent work where people feel free to grow by focusing on their good and goodness, their motivation shifts from external to internal. Their capacity for growth expands and deepens. Their sense of engagement makes work a source of meaning, community and joy.

Beautiful conversations

One of the most significant shapers of team culture is the quality of our conversations. In growing together, nimble teams prefer conversations to meetings.

Slow teams have an interesting, sometimes absurd, faith in meetings. They keep hoping meetings can be productive even though they regularly lament that in most of them no real work gets done.

People in slow cultures believe that unproductive and unengaging meetings happen when there isn't someone at the head of the table keeping people in compliance to an assigned agenda. The implication nimble teams would find bizarre is the idea that meetings derail when people talk about what really matters to them.

It's a problem of geometry. In slow cultures, meetings are triangles. One person decides what people can talk about, for how long and where. In a triangle, there is a top and bottom. Power is divided. When power is divided, the power have-nots bring little of themselves to the table. The vast majority of people attending triangle meetings bring other work, and most of those expect that at some point they will actually fall asleep.

Conversations in nimble cultures are circles. In a circle there is no top or bottom. Power is shared. They have beautiful conversations. People show up. Things get done. Everyone experiences them as fruitful, insightful and enjoyable.

Corporate-speak for meetings and conversations includes the vocabulary of planning, decision making, deliberating, status reporting, problem solving, conflict management, coaching, designing, analyzing and organizing. Any can be a triangle meeting or circle conversation.

That we structure them as formal meetings doesn't necessarily make them productive and satisfying. Most people find beautiful conversations far more conducive to velocity and engagement.

Beautiful conversations go well because people are thinking, not just talking, together. Talking together is not necessarily thinking together.

Talking together is the transaction of knowns, as what happens in status reporting, lecturing, gossip, debating and entertaining. It can be enjoyable because it cocoons us in a world of certainties. As much as talking together can be comforting in a world of uncertainties, it is not necessarily productive or engaging.

Productive is moving from ambiguity to clarity. In thinking together, we move through conversational spaces guided by shared, interesting questions we explore together.

Conversations are beautiful when they are explorations inspired by iterations of shared and new questions.

The difference between conclusion and discovery is that in conclusion, we end curiosity. In discovery, we end in curiosity. The point of conclusions is the end of questions. The point of discovery is openness to the next wave of new questions.

Thinking together is useful when we have a shared problem, puzzle, predicament or possibility to explore. It both engages us in beautiful conversations and creates new levels of engagement beyond the conversations themselves.

Conversation habits

Beautiful conversations go well because we practice conversation habits that make them productive and enjoyable. Not every conversation features all habits. We engage the ones we need when we need them.

Hosting

Hosting is inviting people as inviters around shared questions that matter to everyone. Anyone invited feels free to invite others and offer their questions as well.

Check ins

We find out what everyone is up to, needs help with and wants to offer help. This keeps momentum on anything in progress and needing to get started or completed. People feel valued and valuable.

Understanding a situation

We share all of our current knowns and questions to understand any situation that needs some kinds of resolution, reflection, action or planning. We feel smarter together and better prepared to make good possible.

Generating ideas

We spark and grow ideas for a decision, action or plan.
We start this in a commons before the conversation
and use the conversation to keep evolving, editing and
connecting ideas. We feel proactive and energized.

Deciding

Framing all decisions as single or multiple questions,
we make decisions by shuffling and reshuffling through
the decision quad of all the knowns, unknowns, hopes
and concerns we have related to the decision. We feel
continuously aligned and ultimately focused on good.

Planning

Knowing the good we seek, we together sequence
exactly what will be done, by whom, starting and
finishing when. We tweak plans in real time to stay
responsive to shifting plan landscapes. We feel in sync
and agile.

Reflecting

We extract lessons from experience, efforts and
experiments. We reflect on the success, progress and
their causes. We decide what we would try differently in
the future. We feel a sense of mutual appreciation and
growth.

We can decide which habits to engage in conversations when we invite them, as the begin or as they unfold. For optimal engagement it's important that we decide this together. No one decides this for those participating in conversations.

The craft of engaging conversations

In nimble groups, anyone can invite a conversation, anytime, about anything. No one postpones conversations in a slow culture of permissions and approvals.

We work with an agreement that scheduled conversation inviters post the invitation in the commons as a question or set of questions so anyone can see it and respond. They post how much time they have for the conversation. Others post how much time they have so everyone's time is optimized.

We begin conversations by gathering everyone's questions and checking in to see if anyone thinks someone else needs to be involved.

If there are more than one or two organizing questions we decide if there is a logical order or clustering of questions to work on. We decide who wants to work on which questions and question clusters and depending on how much time everyone has, we work through as much as we can.

It sounds messy but it works. The questions keep focus, momentum and engagement. Getting through the organizing questions could take one short conversation or multiple longer ones, by everyone present or others.

It is not possible to know how long any conversation will take. We can know exactly how long conversations will take the minute they're done.

What people in nimble teams know from experience is that as self-organizing and emergent these kinds of conversations are, they are far more productive and enjoyable than the wasteful and painful meetings in slow teams.

Whether conversations are local, virtual or otherwise, there is a scientifically proven way to keep engagement and productivity high from beginning to end. It's using note cards. People do their best expressive and reflective thinking when they incorporate writing their own ideas into the process.

For an engaging and nimble process, where we are actually smarter and better together, we never have one person control the marker, no matter how smart or important they or others think they are.

We make sure everyone records everything they think and say. People write then speak or speak then write, always one contribution per card making it easier to organize them into action later. Having people working in small units of 2, 3 or 4 people accelerates momentum and yields richer possibilities than anything a larger discussion could ever produce.

Ideas and contributions made visible literally gets and keeps the group on the same page as much as talking into the air weakens collaboration, productivity and creativity.

This approach reduces and eliminates dominating, disappearing and derailing. It keeps everyone optimally engaged and the outcomes pleasing.

New conversations

One of the more salient differences between nimble and slow teams is in the novelty of their conversations.

Slow cultures have mostly old conversations, shaped by old questions. Everyone knows where the conversation is going to go. Eyes roll. Phones emerge.

As soon as an old conversation begins, two things happen: people whose agenda is to avoid more work are happy to replay old scripts and people who want something new check out.

Nimble teams favor new conversations inspired by new questions. No one knows where they will go. New conversations energize interest, engagement and new insights.

We invite new conversations with simple questions:

- Where is our curiosity about this now?
- What should we be talking about now?
- Should we be talking about anything else before this?

Shared decisions, made simple

Shared decision making is one of the most accessible and significant ways people feel valued, connected and free in their work and growth. It accelerates, broadens and deepens growing and trust. When people feel entrusted with decisions, they act trustworthy. People who don't feel trusted, do not feel obligated to be trustworthy.

Decisions can be ideal opportunities for people to show up with integrity, inclusion and initiative.

The process can be simple, engaging, efficient and productive if it is based on the realities that none of us is as smart as all of us and people support what they help create.

We begin by deciding together what the organizing questions for the decision are. We identify who needs to be involved. We clarify who will make final decisions and by when.

There are three kinds of people valuable to decisions: those most knowledgeable about the decision context, those who will be most directly impacted by it and those fluent in thinking together.

Using note cards for everyone to capture each of their contributions, people describe every kind of known, unknown, hope and concern they have related to the decision on the table. Anything sparking debate or spinning discussion becomes a new question.

Where unknowns require some kind of clarification or research, this is done as quickly as possible. Each iteration of conversation leads to progression toward realistic decisions supported by all.

The alchemical synergy of knowns, unknowns, hopes and concerns makes possible organic movement from ambiguity to clarity and action. We grow decisions together. Without the divisiveness of voting and the anxiety of consensus, the process gets us aligned in the wisest approaches possible.

Nimble teams grow, one good decision made together at a time.

Push and pull cultures

When it comes to fostering everyday growth, nimble teams are more predominantly pull cultures. Slow teams are more predominantly push cultures. Both approaches have significant impacts on the growth potentials of teams and organizations.

In a push culture, the expectation is that people with information are primarily responsible for the flow of information they have. It is typical in top-down, centralized and command-control organizations. It emphasizes the slow culture bias that people should know what they have permission to know.

In a push culture, information owners easily disappoint others by not knowing who needs and wants their information, when, how and why.

Because of this, others naturally feel they never get enough or get too much information. It's the feast of fire hydrants or a famine of trickle down. The bloated use of email and meetings are prime tools in and indicators of slow, push cultures.

In a pull culture, the expectation is that people with questions are primarily responsible for the flow of information they want and need. People get information they want and need when, how and why they do. It is hardly a slow culture of waiting and wondering, where formal information moves at the speed of drying paint while gossip flashes at the speed of lightning.

In a pull culture, people with information get better at assessing how to share information because they discover through questions what people need to know, when, how and why. People get just the right amount of information that works for them.

In nimble, pull cultures, transparency becomes more relevant. People with information can still share what they have in useful ways. The commons makes the right balance of relevant pull and push more possible.

Moving from a push to pull culture makes for the most efficient and high engagement approach possible. Active question creators are always more engaged than passive information consumers.

Question based status conversations

Pull cultures thrive in question based status conversations.

When it's each person's turn to report out, everyone else is invited to say what they're interested in hearing and reporters address these questions and then fill in with anything else they feel it's important to share that wasn't asked for. Everyone gets better at anticipating and responding to what people want to know.

Question based posted reports

When anyone is preparing a report to post or share, they invite everyone to post in a dedicated virtual space any related questions they have. Report creators rely on these questions to shape and structure the report.

Question based open forums

A shared space for each leader, coordinator and project manager is created where people at any time can post any questions they have for these leaders, coordinators or project managers.

Question based one-on-ones

We start these conversations with pre-shared or shared in the moment questions for each other, including the contexts of why each question matters to us. The more specific they are the better.

Who's responsible for a teams's growth?

People on nimble teams feel and act like they are the ultimate authors of their destiny. Their velocity, tenacity and productivity happens because they do not outsource this responsibility to parent figures, no matter how talented or charming they might be. People in slow teams outsource responsibility for their work and growth to their leaders.

The most profound way leaders get in the way of growth is by acting like they're responsible for people. It doesn't matter that their leaders are complicit in holding them responsible for others. Nothing slows down a teams more than a leader who feels responsible for them and communicates this in word or attitude.

Leaders do this in subtle and not so subtle ways. They dictate meeting times, agendas and invitations according to what works for them. They deliver unilateral feedback to people when and how it's convenient for them.

They make themselves the final word on anything of significance. They act entitled to all kinds of advantages and freedoms no one on the team equally enjoys. They decide how people and things will improve. They act like they're in a protected and privileged class.

As a result, people act with less sense of responsibility for their performance and growth. They feel obligated to view taking responsibility for themselves as disloyalty and disrespect to their permission-holding leaders.

90% of change management programs in slow organizations fail. This is not a mystery when we understand that people only grow when they feel responsible together for their growth.

No one has to put nimble people through change management. No one has to sign up to champion their transformation. Their growth is continuous and unstoppable because they know how to make growth the point of work.

Rethinking power

People and teams cannot grow in a command and control atmosphere. They are not free to take initiative in a two class system of power haves and have-nots. Freedom to grow is core to capacity for growth.

Most leaders in these environments have not yet developed the ability to transfer decision making to their teams.

This transition to shared power does not need to be the quick or slow pain of pulling off a bandaid. It does not need to create anywhere near intolerable uncertainty levels.

It optimally happens one decision at a time, starting ideally with easier ones. The decision making leader finds out who wants to develop the ability to participate in any standing or anticipated decision. The leader then coaches the volunteers through the development of competency with this decision.

The coaching begins with sharing stories of past experiences of this decision, in reflective critique of what when well and why and how each experience might have featured some kind of new abilities, or at least ones that went well.

The leader then, with a live or upcoming decision, walks them through their decision quad: knowns, unknowns, hopes and concerns. They dialogue on process options and the leader guides them to a viable approach the leader then takes.

Leaders shares their experiences, adjustments and insights along the way, making especially transparent their thought process throughout. These sharings are based on the volunteers' questions. After the decision, the leader and volunteers do a final reflection and explore implications of what the post-decision good could be.

How leaders can grow and how we can help

There are many new abilities leaders can create that directly support people growing together.

They can create a new ability to support a culture where people feel valued, connected and free to grow.

We can help by inviting conversations where we share how we've been seeing people engage their goodness in work. We can model and invite working from presence, promises and agreements. We can make sure we all know what everyone's working on and that we have things we're all working on together.

They can create a new ability to guide people in making decisions together they used to make.

We can offer to volunteer to develop the know how to take over especially reactive decisions that free up their time to be more proactive.

They can create a new ability to give and ask for useful perspective.

We can show them how to talk about what we're working on, ask for useful perspectives and ask what they're working on and if they would like our perspectives and if so how, when and why.

They can create a new ability to engage us in being proactive.

We can raise proactive questions and invite them to work together on learning our way into the future.

They can create a new ability to move from the hubris of thinking they have to know all the answers to the humility of being more curious than certain.

We can remind them that it takes many or all of us to see any picture in its entirety, that's it's really OK for any of us to have more questions than answers. We can help by making the culture more of a nimble, pull culture where having questions is golden.

The Future of Growth

The unreasonable power of the future

When it comes to how we grow in the present, there is mounting evidence that our sense of the future is more significant than our sense of the past. The more clarity we have in narrating the future we want to see, the more we grow in the present.

It is no coincidence that when we imagine a future that lights us up, we begin noticing new ways to make meaningful progress in the present. Fewer new possibilities reveal themselves in rear view mirrors.

This makes the past a more irrelevant hitchhiker's guide to our galaxy of unpredictable possibilities. In a world that rewards the nimble, how we reimagine our future will always have more power than how we remember our past. When it comes to the past, what can inspire a new future is discovering new aspects of the past.

Our sense of the future animates and focuses the mindful present. When we want to reshape our sense of the present, we need to reshape our clarity about the future.

The Agile Canvas conversations

Crafting our most desirable and possible future happens in the synergy of four dynamic conversations: dreaming, clarity, gifts and doing.

Dreaming

In the dreaming conversation, we describe what we want to see and make possible. We go out as far as we can and keep translating everything into what progress would look like. In strategic, business and community planning we start by going out one generation of 20 years. We prioritize our dreams according to which need to happen before others.

The depth of new possibilities in the present is equal to the length of our vision of the future we seek. This gives us inspiration and focus. Turning dream statements into questions give them 3-5 times more power.

As our world changes and we change it, we refresh our dreams on a regular cadence, for example every two quarters. Success is progress toward the latest versions of the dreams we have energy and alignment for.

Clarity

In the clarity conversation, we identify anything unknown, unconfirmed and undecided relative to our dreams. We translate everything into questions that we prioritize and move to as much clarity as we can. The whole process moves at the tempo we move from ambiguity to clarity. This gives the process realistic expectations.

As the process unfolds, new questions keep emerging and we schedule and act on them accordingly.

Gifts

We identify every kind of goodness and resources we have available at the table that can support our priority dream progress and clarity questions.

With dreams and questions identified, it's more clear who else we should invite into the effort. We invite them to join us in making progress on our dreams and clarity. This gives the process collaboration and velocity.

Doing

In the doing conversation, we outline, timestamp and sign up for what we will do every two weeks to make progress toward our dreams and clarity from our questions. We refresh the whole outline every two weeks considering what we achieve and discover along the way. This gives the process traction and agility.

These are the four conversations of the Agile Canvas. They can be used for any scope of planning and organization, with any number of participants, over any period of time, addressing any possible issues and priorities.

The conversations are dynamically interrelated. They can occur in any order because new work in any one creates implications for the others. Everything we do in doing can shift our sense of the good we dream, the clarity we further need and who else we need to engage. When we use it in planning, the "plan" is to continuous work in and from the four conversations.

Mindful trending

The more mindful we are in shaping and realizing our future, the more fluidly we balance responsive and proactive.

Harvard researcher Ellen Langer describes mindfulness as knowing what's new in our world. The key to balancing being responsive and proactive is tracking what's going on in our world beyond our mindless assumptions. We do this in our clarity conversations.

With change as life's constant, trends are always emerging and shifting. Tracking trends means doing whatever research, observing and assumption testing on what's happening with those who rely on the value we deliver and what's happening in their worlds.

It's keeping up with what's happening in our industries and professions. It's keeping up with the kind of talent graduates schools are releasing into our workforces.

It's staying conscious of the larger social, political and technological trends that ultimately shape the world we work within and from.

Being more mindful about our markets means continuously tracking what's happening in the markets we serve and the markets that impact them.

Tracking means compassionate clarity about where people are improving and succeeding, struggling and pivoting. They are the reason we have value. To know our potential is to know theirs.

Mindfulness is our way of doing business to the extent it's clear that unpredictability is the new predictability. We can no longer afford to rely on prediction, guessing, debating and discussion as a substitute for continuous curiosity and discovery. This is being clear on the difference between estimating and exploring.

Being mindfully responsive and proactive reveals possibilities we cannot possibly anticipate, however successful we have been or are, no matter how smart we think we are or reactive we try to be. We cannot guess or react our way into a new future.

Creating the future we want to see is not about our ability to predict it but our ability to inquire and grow into it.

Recovering our creativity potential

Growing the future is engagement of our creative potentials. Everything amazing today that would have been utterly unpredictable twenty years ago came about because nimble people came together in creativity.

This is a call for recovering our creative potential. The key word here is recovering. We are born creative. Our brains are hardwired for curiosity, awe and making new connections between previously unconnected impressions. This is all creativity is.

In early childhood, we use about 80% of our creativity potential. Conventional education reduces this to less than 10% by age 12 because our young brains atrophy as academic and developmental success is measured more in compliant certainty than cultivated curiosity.

Thanks to the neuroplastic nature of our brains, we can reawaken our dormant creative potential at any point in our life.

We can grow any creative form that appeals to us. It can be in any form of writing, drawing, painting, photography, studio arts, film, music, cooking, gardening or design. These are now all possible mostly with the cost of time. We can use our creativity to navigate life's constant of change. The potential is unlimited.

It is not uncommon to find people on nimble teams who have all kinds of creative expressions and practices in their lives. Just dedicating ourselves to growing in our work as art and craft restores and reengages our creativity. Everything gets better: our dreams and goodness, our kindness and conversations, our growth and significance.

The magic of constraints

Until we learn how to be intentionally creative together, we feel frustrated and victimized by constraints. Constraints are conditions we cannot, at this time, change. There are always budget, staffing, time, contract, work rules, power, politics and regulatory constraints.

Nimble teams have as many constraints as slow teams, and if we don't, we often create new constraints for ourselves knowing that love of constraints actually makes us more creative. We don't get confused about them, assuming they have power to limit creativity.

A constraint can be a condition supporting the creative process. Not only can we get creative around constraints, adding constraints can stimulate new possibilities.

We can begin idea sessions with a blue sky of no constraints or with a set of constraints. Both have distinct power to evoke and provoke new questions and options.

Researching the plethora of brilliant stories of creative breakthroughs in any discipline today reveals how people discover new approaches in spite of, and often because of the real constraints they had to deal with or chose for creative purposes to work within for new possibilities.

Simply refusing to see constraints as immutable obstacles puts us in a more creative space together.

The vitality and value of unrealistic ideas

One of the hallmark indicators of creativity is how ideas are welcome to the dynamic mix, realistic or not. The assessment of realistic and unrealistic is based on untested assumptions about what's possible in the present and future. If people refused to work on ideas considered possibly unrealistic, we would likely have few of the innovations we enjoy today.

Unrealistic simply means we haven't yet discovered how to make something work. Having unknowns doesn't guarantee non-feasibility. No amount of risk aversion and change resistance sums up to accurate prediction in the value of an idea, especially as it begins to emerge.

Unrealistic ideas are vital to the creative process, even and especially in shared creative work sessions. It's no coincidence that teams manage to generate the most uninspired and cliched ideas as they strive to come up with realistic ideas that aren't criticism and rejection magnets.

It's also no coincidence that so many of the best ideas on the planet originated in forms that would seem to most reasonable people as unreasonable. Much of the best features of our world today represent what would not long ago have been judged as impossible by experts and clueless alike.

We are in large measure more creative, alone and together, when we let all the unrealistic ideas we can generate, spark and seed new ideas.

Growing ideas

Ideas are living things. Everything they encounter helps them flourish or fail.

Ideas grow in supportive conversational environments that feature 5 idea nutrients of inquiry, dependencies, expansions, affirmation and synthesis.

Inquiry is asking for more details to better understand the features, functions and implications of ideas. Dependencies are all the things that need to happen before an idea becomes viable. Expansions are features and functions to add to an idea to make it stronger or more viable. Affirmation is what we like about an idea that gives it potential usefulness. Synthesis is the both-and of how we could optimize the upsides and minimize the downsides of two or more opposing ideas.

Inquiry

So can you tell us more about this idea? Every idea raises questions. We want to know about who, what, when, where, how, why. We want to know what if and what about.

Curiosity is the opposite of judgment. It is a space of presence. Ideas grow in the present, not in the past or future.

More questions lead to better questions. There are better questions but we can't judge any question until we see what it leads to. It's just important that we don't reject questions.

People often have more in mind than they initially express. The more details we get, the more we can help ideas grow. The more we detail what an idea could be like, the more clearly we become on the potentials of the idea. This is why it's important to ask what else people can tell us about any idea.

Dependencies

When could this idea happen, given what needs to come before? In ideas, as in life, timing is everything.

Many times the difference between a good idea and a less good idea is timing. An idea is good if it is useful. An idea is useful when its time is right. An idea that appears to be good but is ahead of or behind its time is not useful.

Having a sense of timing gets us considering what else if anything needs to occur for this idea to work. We might discover that we need to put many new things in place first in order for a potentially good idea to work.

Asking what would need to happen before this illuminates prerequisites.

We cannot always know exactly when an idea can become reality. We can make estimates that split the difference between our most optimistic and pessimistic scenarios. The larger and more novel an idea, the more previous steps it will require.

Because an idea can't work today doesn't guarantee it also won't in the future. The idea for a laptop before the typewriter era would have been labelled unworkable, but possible once a typewriter and a thousand other ideas would come to fruition first.

Expansions

What could we add to make this idea stronger? We can add another element, feature or dimension. We can add a twist to it. We can add another way to make it more functional, realistic or feasible in our context.

The addition can be small or large. It can be within or beyond our scope of resources and capabilities. We think of minimal viable products. What could be the simplest version, given our current resources and capabilities, that could allow us to try it, experiment with it and prototype it?

Many new living things have fragile and undeveloped embryonic beginnings. We don't discard them for not popping out mature. We strengthen them along the way to vitality and value.

Affirmation

What do we like about this idea? Every idea has some benefit, some advantage, some upside. We don't have to like all of it. We don't have to agree with it completely. We simply acknowledge its potential value.

When we declare what we like about an idea, people with the idea feel heard. When people feel heard they no longer feel urgency to defend and protect it. They become open to learning about it, from it and beyond it. Ideas grow best when people feel welcome to voice their ideas without self-editing and self-filtering. We are more generative together when we are more relaxed together.

New ideas do not grow when we feel we have to be on the defensive. We put each other on the defensive when our first reaction to any idea is questioning, pushing back, attacking its validity or pointing out its obvious deficiencies and risks. The parts of our brain involved in creativity, passion and clear decision making shut down when we go into judgment mode.

When we identify anything we like about an idea, what we like gives shape to other possibilities. We build on what we like. Like is the foundation for new differences to consider. We can grow an idea we like in some way. We can start to think of other alternatives and variations.

Synthesis

How else could we realize the advantages and minimize the disadvantages of this idea? Every idea on the planet has upside and downsides depending on their use contexts and how we define good.

Downsides are not reasons to abandon the essential good of the idea. They are problems and puzzles to research and solve. They are calls to prototyping alternatives and variations.

When either-or and conflicting ideas emerge, synthesis is generating what we could do, given our resources and capabilities, to make upsides more possible and downsides less possible. The best way forward is the synergy of approaches that we together create. We discover the wisdom and power of both-and.

Growing ideas through these five nutrients is a practice of kindness in the creation of beauty.

Design HUBS

Design is a juicy opportunity for creativity and innovation. Everything in our world works exactly as it was designed to perform. If we want anything to function better we need to redesign it. This is why we're reimagining the future of work.

Design HUBS are work sessions dedicated to the design or redesign of anything. It can be the design of any kind of product, service, process, program, event or experience.

It engages four elements: habits, use, beauty and sense making. Together these nurture the organic growth of design that works. The power of the process is how it engages every thinking style and talent around the table.

Habits

What are people already doing?

Whatever we're designing or redesigning for, people are already doing. Before Post-It Notes, people were attaching paper to paper using paper clips and staples. Post-Its brought about a completely different feature for the same function, replacing sturdy solid materials with inferior glue.

New design gives people a different way to do what they're already doing. Here, we study what for users is working and not working, what's most and least convenient, what adds value and what doesn't. Understanding current habits gives us a unique and deeper perspective on what else might be useful.

Use

What features and functions would be optimally useful?

We create usefulness by making something more accessible, functioning with fewer steps, producing a higher quality experience, requiring minimal or no maintenance, easy to personalize or share, at less expense in production or maintenance.

We generate as many feature and function possibilities, no matter how much we might judge them as "realistic" or "unrealistic." We consider interesting ways to introduce any kinds of smart technology and savvy sociology into the options that emerge.

The test for usefulness is actual user performance and experience in an experiment, pilot or prototype. It's not debating our opinions or accumulating more opinion support from others. Idea testing is about data vetting not democratic voting. It's clarity more than consensus.

Beauty

What would make this more beautiful?

Beauty is not something we add to design. It is a principle in the whole of design. Just the question of beauty infuses our process with greater attention to the details of value.

Beauty is aesthetics in use and use in aesthetics. Anything judged as attractive feels more useful and representing higher quality. Beauty has a symbolic dimension, enticing us to assume that more attention went into the design and production of something.

Just considering the beauty of something we design adds another perspective on the importance of the user experience, which infuses more creativity and pragmatism to the overall value of the design.

Sense making

What useful insights has our experience given us?

At the heart of growing good design is agnostic testing and deep critique.

Agnostic testing is prototyping design options with actual users in actual contexts. It's agnostic because we aren't trying to prove or disprove a hypothesis or bias. We're assessing for habit, use and beauty with an open mindset of sheer curiosity.

Deep critique is getting behind what we discover. It's a relentless and compassionate attitude of why. We want to know why things are and aren't useful and beautiful. We resist the impatient and defensive temptation to react into problem solving. We don't as much decide how to proceed. We let reality lead the way. We create design that has a timeless significance.

Who can improve an industry?

The conversation about disruptive technologies is the conversation about industry disruption.

Cars replace horses, electricity replaces human efforts, internet replaces mail, robots replace repetitive human tasks, automated vehicles replace drivers, sharing replaces ownership, smart phones replace in person socializing, learning and shopping.

Social currencies replace institutional currencies, machine intelligence replaces highest levels professional work in medicine, law and education. When it comes to future industry transformations, there is no end in sight.

These transformations weren't necessarily the domain of industry giants or geniuses. Many began at the margins of industries and in the open source spaces of networks between them. Some of the most significant came from nimble teams of industry newbies and outliers

Perhaps the most salient factor is how these industry innovations begin in the profound shift in questions from how can we make business as usual better to how can we reinvent or replace our industry with something totally else, before someone else does.

Nimble teams can work from a passion for growing their organization and their industry. The desire to change our industry uniquely empowers our growth as an organization. The future of industry disruption and adaptation to it belongs to the nimble.

Ambivalence about innovation

While over 90% of executives believe innovation is key to their company's success, half actually invest in ways to make it happen. Many don't know how. This is across the board of corporations, school and hospital systems, NGOs and government organizations.

Most executives today were raised in slow organizations where early growth is measured in investments and later growth is measured in acquisitions.

Senior leaders still need to talk about innovation if for no other reason than to assuage the worries of their boards, investors and funders.

Those serious about innovation will do whatever they can to help their teams move from slow to nimble. They don't have to engineer elaborate and expensive programs that in the end make innovation more slow than nimble.

Innovation has never flourished in approval based programs. It thrives in the accidental and beautiful conversations of nimble teams and networks.

The change-growth distinction

As much as we invest in failing change management programs, not all change is growth. We can change leaders, talent, goals, resources, constraints, metrics, incentives, accountabilities, roles, systems, structures and processes. We can create change that doesn't result in growth, and effectively prevents it. All we have to do is impose changes that have nothing to do with growing together.

The kind of change that promotes growth is change people create. People responsible for their own change are constantly adapting and improvising what they do and how they do it from their rich ecology of growth and trust.

People growing together discover how to create changes that make them smarter, faster and better together. These are changes that bring out their best in the direction of what they define as good.

The sociology of spreading change for good

When nimble teams stumble on or rigorously innovate some new way of working, they are eager to see it organically spread it across teams and the organization.

This kind of natural contagion does not happen by top-down mandates spammed in emails, announcements, town halls or training rollouts. If anything, each command and control effort makes people feel less freedom in their work, leading to lower levels of performance and culture. It is not a realistic approach.

What works is leveraging the natural power of networks. In spite of what organization charts imply, organization are networks of people and teams. In every network there are three kinds of responses to anything new.

There are early, middle and later adopters. Interestingly, there tend to be more connections between early and middle adopters than early and later adopters. What's equally important and useful is that middle adopters start to trust and engage in something new when they see interest and enthusiasm from the early adopters with whom they have trust connections.

Spreading anything new means putting all initial efforts into identifying and engaging early adopters and helping them invite their middle adopter connections. No resources are squandered on trying to convert later adopters before engaging early and middle adopters. As early adopters get engaged, we adapt design for their delight.

If we scientifically map the networks of people potentially engaged, we can mathematically identify the network weavers, the people best positioned to connect people. This accelerates progress, success and spread. This how change has always worked since the beginning of human experience.

People want to be nimble

Aside from an inconsolable margin of people in organizations who prefer slow for their own self-serving reasons, most people want to be nimble. We love growing and growing together. We love that work can be a rich context for growing and being nimble.

We don't want to waste even small windows of our careers in a culture of permission, focusing on everything wrong about us and everyone else.

We long to feel valued, connected and free to grow. We long to create and sustain a culture where growth is more delight than a reminder of our inadequacies. We long for work that makes us better for all the people and causes we care most about in our lives.

We don't have to be coerced or converted into being nimble. Nimble is its own reward.

Nimble is an easy mindset to grow into. We already have the goodness required. As radically different as it might be in slow organizations, we have experienced nimble in a variety of life contexts. All we need is to dedicate ourselves to it in our work.

Nimble transitions

Making the transition from slower to more nimble team cultures is hardly linear. Each team finds and makes its own way.

Each way differs depending on a mix of variables: how slow or nimble the team is to start with, how much experience outside work people have had with being on nimble teams, how slow and nimble people tend to be in their lives, how ready people are to make progress in the direction of more nimble and, if they have a leader, how prepared their leader is to support the transition.

Wherever we begin the transition to being a more nimble team is the right place to begin. Every team already has exactly what it needs for progress.

The shift is a shift from business as usual practices of goals and roles, emails and meetings, performance reviews and power divisions. Each is an exercise in the confusion of slow that prevents the nimble of growing together.

Here are a dozen new practices to get started with:

1. **Agile Canvas**: Launch an Agile Canvas for any aspect of work as a team
2. **Progress**: Translate goals now in place into realistic, clear progress indicators
3. **Goodness**: Do goodness mapping with everyone on the team, optimally through story sharing
4. **Growing questions**: invite people to identify and share their growing questions

5. **Sync**: Create sync with more engagement in a commons
6. **Creativity**: Introduce growing ideas and design HUBS in any work sessions
7. **Conversations**: Move meetings to conversations and more conversations to the commons
8. **Conversation habits**: Introduce and practice the conversation habits
9. **Grow the commons**: Move emails, documents and updates to the commons
10. **Pull**: Move push communication to pull with question based conversations
11. **Deepen connections**: Start shared kindness, perspectives and sense making conversations
12. **Smarter together**: Move some of everyday work from roles to being smarter together with initiative, inclusion and integrity.

In each use context, we might be paving new paths in our organization but not new paths in the world. We might be pioneers, but we are not alone.

At the margins of slow organizations and in entrepreneurial workplaces, teams have been working from the growth imperative for decades. More organizations are finally ready to move out of the industrial age into an age of consciousness.

This transition epitomizes growth. It's all about experimenting and tweaking. It's all about the momentum of progress toward the team we want to see.

The shift in culture is often immediate and always palpable. No one needs formal assessments or tests to measure the shifts. It's abundantly obvious to everyone. We thrive in the land of nimble.

Growing our way into the future

The future belongs to the nimble. When we are nimble, we know the future we get is the future we create. When our work is about being aspired, responsive and connected, we grow our way into the future we seek.

When we move from slow to more nimble, we open up to clarity that uncertainty is a precious gift.

Each day we show up with our goodness in our work, we don't know what kinds of change will greet us. We don't know what our actions will bring. We don't know how our sense of the good we seek will shift.

All that is clear is that if we grow together, we will create beauty from shared dreams. If we do business as unusual, our markets will notice and reward the responsive value we promise and deliver.

Our lives will be better for it. Work will infuse our lives with meaning and significance. Our communities will flourish. Our world will transform in the ubiquity of uncertainty. Our ever expanding clarity will make it all possible.

This the growth imperative awaiting us.

Gratitude

For the making of the book, I want to express deep gratitude to friends and practice partners Jen Margolis and Doug Craver who inspire new vistas on growth, in their wisdom and lives.

Thanks again to cover diva, Tia, for making this yet another book that will sell by the cover.

About the Author

Jack Ricchiuto has been helping organizations reimagine the future of work and communities globally in 24+ industries, over 40 years of workshops and coaching, inspired by 22 books.

He is the originator of the groundbreaking planning model, The Agile Canvas and co-founder and partner with Thrive At Work.

Jack has been honored to work with entrepreneurs and Fortune 500s, aboriginal tribal leaders and executive teams, doctors and educators, organic farmers and tech innovators, funders and investors, nonprofits and grass roots groups, government leaders and scientists, designers and innovators.

...

For book orders and inquiries on how to bring the growth imperative to your organization, visit TheGrowthImperative.co